Reflections
OF A BUSINESS NOMAD

Reflections
OF A **BUSINESS NOMAD**
stories & poems from the road

PASCAL DENNIS

Skopelos Press

Skopelos Press

Division of Zero Loss Quality Systems Inc.

660 Eglinton Avenue East

Suite 119-539

Toronto, ON

Canada M4G-2K2

P: 416-424-3056; E: info@skopelospress.com

W: skopelospress.com; reflections-of-a-business-nomad.com

ISBN-13: 978-0-987778-60-4

LCCN: 2012910136

Distributed by Itasca Books

Cover and interior artwork by Kirk Sutterfield

www.kirksindustrialarts.com

Cover Design and Typeset by Sophie Chi

Printed in the United States of America

Also by Pascal Dennis

*The Remedy – Bringing Lean Out of the Factory
to Transform the Entire Organization*

*Getting the Right Things Done – a Leader's
Guide to Strategy Deployment*

Andy & Me – Crisis & Transformation on the Lean Journey

*Lean Production Simplified – a Plain Language Guide
to the World's Most Powerful Production System*

Quality, Safety & Environment – Synergy in the 21st Century

For Pamela

Table of Contents

DRAWINGS

Acknowledgments

I'm grateful to all the good people who have helped to make this book a reality, and acknowledge them here:

Allen Sutterfield, my writing sensei, for his patience and light touch. Kirk Sutterfield, for his splendid drawings. Michael Brassard and Al Norval, for their friendship and perceptive feedback. All our reviewers, for their time and care. The Skopelos Press and Hillcrest Media Group teams for their support. The Lean Pathways team, and our friends and colleagues at client companies, with whom it is our privilege to work.

Special thanks to all my senseis over the years who have done so much for me.

Last, but not least, my dear wife, Pamela, and our children, Eleanor, Katie, and Matthew.

Preface

It is circumstances, difficulties, which show what people are.
Epictetus

I make my living on the road, teaching the Toyota Way. It's an odd life—sensei, scholar, stand-up comedian—but one I've chosen and very much enjoy. These pieces were written in airports, restaurants, and hotel bars. There are benefits to writing when you're tired. You're open to things you might otherwise shut down.

Why is a management consultant writing prose poetry?

My mother taught me poetry is storytelling. At bedtime she'd recite the adventures of Captain Kanaris, Bouboulina, and Odysseus (my favorite) in rhyming couplets. I know some good stories and wanted to set them down. The medium seemed natural.

Why did I write *this* book?

We live in tough times. I'd like to help shift contemporary business discourse, in some small way, toward the cardinal virtues—Prudence, Temperance, Justice, and Courage—and the great virtues[1] in general.

We *can* remake ourselves. I work with people at every level who act with decency and courage, often in bleak circumstances. These pieces are dedicated to them.

_____

1   Readers interested in the great virtues are directed to *A Small Treatise on the Great Virtues* (New York: Henry Holt, 1996) by Andre Comte-Sponville.

No-mad

– noun

1. *a member of a people or tribe that has no permanent abode but moves from place to place, usually seasonally and often following a traditional route according to the state of the pasturage or food supply.*

2. *any wanderer, itinerant.*

Re-flec-tion

– noun

1. *an image given back from a reflecting surface.*

2. *attentive or continued consideration, contemplation, or meditation.*

Company names have been avoided in this volume. Where necessary to preserve confidentiality, the industry and/or geography have been changed.

I. FORTITUDE

Meeting Buzz Aldrin in Fort Worth

Eyes bright as solar flares,
hair silver as the Orion Nebula,
almost eighty now
still a bantamweight,
he talks to us about his dream:
"A Mission to Mars, a permanent colony!"

Fighter pilot in Korea,
Doctorate in physics (MIT),
the second man to walk the moon.
Survivor: a mother's suicide, alcoholism, two divorces.
He even found time to thump that conspiracy creep.[1]

Third wife beside him today
California gal with a cheerful wrinkled face
(*"She pulled me back to Earth . . ."*).

He flies around the world advocating space exploration
to Russians, Chinese, Indians.
He files patents for space station design.

---

1   (http://www.youtube.com/watch?v=ZOo6aHSY8hU).

He can't fathom apathy before the stars.

"Why not a manned colony on the *moon*?" someone asks.

"The moon's an awful place! No atmosphere, no water, all that radiation . . ."

It occurs to me, he's *been* there.

"Why a *permanent* Martian colony?" another asks.

"The journey takes two years. After that the orbits don't coincide for another three. So, you might as well stay."

It's hard to argue with him!

Chat done, we gather round for pictures
with our modern-day Odysseus.
Afterward, someone says,
"He's not as tall as I thought he'd be."

Summer 2009

Misha

Pearson Airport Terminal 1, another business trip completed. An SUV taxi pulls up. The driver gets out and helps me with my luggage. Blond, blue-eyed, humorous, he looks like a young Gene Wilder. I give him my address. We turn onto HW 401.

I am silent, out of it, digesting my consulting gig. The early evening traffic's heavy but moving well. Then two racers appear, muscle cars careening left and right, accelerating into and out of narrow gaps, narrowly averting disaster.

"Look at those idiots! I have six kids. What would happen if I was killed by such stupidity? You hear about that Indian cabby? He was killed by street racers. I knew him. The poor guy had three kids, he had just dropped off a customer. They hit him as he turned on to Mt. Pleasant. Lots of hills there. He never saw them coming. All the cabbies, we gave money for the family. It was a stupid teenage boy racing his brand new Audi. His father is Russian mafia."

"I heard about it," I reply. "It was near our house. An awful story."

"I'm a photographer, you know. I'd like to set up a video camera on my dashboard and give the evidence to the police. But the courts would say it was INADMISSIBLE. *How stupid can you be? When I came to Canada I thought government would be better, but they are stupid here too."*

He makes a droll face. *"Did you hear about that thief? He is robbing a house, he slips and breaks his arm. So now he is suing the homeowner!"*

I laugh out loud. "Where are you from?"
"Take a guess."
"I'd say Eastern Europe—Russia or the Ukraine."
"I am Ukrainian, from Kiev! How did you know?"
"I have a Ukrainian colleague," I tell him. "His name is Mike."
"Misha—that's my name!"

He's been in Canada for over twenty years, fleeing the Soviet bloc as the Berlin Wall came down. Like my friend Mike, he chose Canada.
"Why not Israel?" I ask.

"All those Jews, they would drive me crazy. Always arguing, fighting, trying to cheat each other. Okay, when there's a war they pull together. Who needs it?"

I ask him about growing up in the Soviet Union.

"The Canadian state is bad, but the Soviet state you cannot imagine. I am Jewish but I have never been to Shabbat. I don't go to the synagogue. It was not a big deal in our family. My mother, her name was Ida, she changed our name from Chernevsky to Chernenko to avoid anti-Semitism. It didn't work . . .

"They don't let you live. When I was in the army, they beat me up every day, especially this one guy named Sergei. He used to call me dirty Jew and beat the hell out of me. So I got strong and one day I beat him up. I knocked him down and sat on him and I said, 'WHY DO YOU HATE ME, SERGEI? WHAT HAVE I EVER DONE TO YOU?'

"And he said, 'YOU'RE A DIRTY JEW. YOU KILL CHRISTIAN CHILDREN AND MAKE MATZO WITH THEIR BLOOD!'

"Can you imagine anything so stupid? So I said, 'Listen, matzo is white, it's just water and flour. How could there be blood in it? Don't be an idiot.'

"But he was just a Ukrainian from the mountains. That's all he knew, to hate the Jews. So I decided to get out."

"How do you like Canada?"

"Not bad. I was hoping there would be more freedom, but it's a lot like the Soviet Union. I am not a right-wing guy, but socialism,

it just doesn't work. At least they don't beat you up here. But you have to act stupid about a lot of things."

"What are your plans, Misha?"

"Well, I have a business and I own my cab. My children are good in school. I didn't get the chance, but they will have it. They will have a chance at a bright future."

He pulls up in front of the house. I am thinking about racers and racists, about his kids and mine. We settle up, shake hands, and I wave as Misha drives off.

True Vermonter

I drove south out of Montreal
into a nor'easter that should've cleared, but didn't.
I crossed into Vermont.
The border guard warned me,
"IT'S A MESS!"

Not far to go, I took a chance
and drove into the high Vermont hills
past the point of no return.

Black night, 2:00 a.m.
listening to the garage rock of my youth,
Little Steven, *Desolation Row.*
Inching along, up a long dark hill,
the only soul on this widowmaker road.

Just past St. Albans, I hit black ice
and slide into the guard rail—*HARD.*
The rental car hangs on the edge of a sheer cliff.

I get out slowly, and walk-slide to the shoulder
to wheels pointing crazy,
the right side of the car crushed.

I stand there with the emergency flashers on
cell phone still alive, wondering who to call . . .

Two lights appear: a monster F-350 with a plow.
Another monster gets out:
heavy, bearded, thick glasses.
"Glad I found ya! Border guy said you'd be in trouble."

He hooks up my car, pulls me out of there.
We work our way along the killer road.
"Every year we lose folks here.
Usually city folk—no offence."

We shoot the breeze an hour, strangers in a maelstrom.
I tell him about my family and business.
He tells me about his ex-wife,
"She cleaned me out. I had to start all over."
and about his business,
"Lots of fly-by-nighters. It's tough to make a go.
I need to get my name out."

He drove me to the hotel—and refused payment.
"Just glad you're okay, man."
He checked back next day and helped me get home.
I sent him a gift on behalf of my wife and kids
and told the story to everybody I met. (Now I'm telling
you.)
To all of those who "hate America"
I offer Larry Lapan.

Greek Tragedy
Ioannina, Greece

He is a world-renowned medical researcher. We are sitting by the green water of Lake Pamvotis, sipping Turkish coffee. In front of us, Justinian's castle and the minaret of Aslan Pasha Mosque; in the distance, the shadowy mountains of Epirus.

A ferry trundles past, taking tourists to the little island in the middle of the lake, where they'll visit the Monastery of St. Panteleimon and the house where Ali Pasha[2] made his last stand.

"You would not believe it. To get an X-ray, I have to argue with the lab. Forget about getting an MRI. I have a private practice, too. My patients all have the same thing: high blood pressure, cholesterol, and hypertension. I prescribe the same three pills. They ask if there's a pill that will make the other

---

2   Ali Pasha ruled the western portion of the Ottoman Empire's European territory. He waged a three-year rebellion against the unpopular Sultan Mahmud II, and was killed by the Sultan's troops in the monastery of St. Panteleimon.

three go away.' EXERCISE,' I tell them. 'THAT'S THE PILL TO MAKE THE OTHERS GO AWAY.'

"I'm most afraid for the young. They want to destroy the current system, to start all over. But they have nothing to offer. They don't work, they don't study. They live at home, smoke cigarettes, and play idiotic computer games all day. One kid brags to me he's NEVER read a book. Can you imagine?

"We're a MIDDLE EAST country! The common good, what's that? Look after your family, and screw everyone else. Our only hope is to cut out the rot—the civil service, the unions, the protected industries. The worst thing would be to go back to the drachma. Our debt would triple overnight and the rot would still be there.

"Some people blame the Turks. Did they destroy the social contract? I don't know. But nobody pays taxes; nobody wants to work. And they want to retire at age fifty-five—with a full pension. LEAVING WAS THE BEST THING YOUR FAMILY EVER DID."

So why do *you* stay, I ask.

"Because I love Greece."

Anthracite

Wyoming Valley, Pennsylvania

He is a tightly-wound third-generation Hunky,[3]
a Plant Manager and Steelers fan.
His wife is dying, and his kids are messed up by it.
Who wouldn't be?
His intensity scares people, but I like the guy.
He's smart, tough, well-read.
Without him, the factory would have been long gone.

This Pennsylvania valley is glorious. The Susquehanna
sparkles,
the Alleghenies play leapfrog into the far distance,
all the way to Pittsburgh and Carnegie's steel mills[4]—or
what's left of them.

"The Homestead and Thompson mills,
they sucked coal out of these hills for a century."

There were both surface and strip mines.
He knows them, and all the graveyards too:

---

3   Slang for people of Hungarian, Czech, or Polish origin.

4   The Carnegie Steel Company was the world's largest and most
profitable company in the late 1800s. Its biggest works were the
Homestead and Thompson mills near Pittsburgh.

"The Knox Mine[5] victims are buried just outside town.
The tombstones all say January 22, 1959.They all drowned,
imagine that.
Got some Molly McGuires[6] buried there too.
Had I lived back then, I'd have joined them!"

We drink in the Banshee, a funeral home turned Irish pub.
"More Irish here than any other U.S. town but Boston!"
Gaelic mugs adorn the walls: WB Yeats, JFK, Van Morrison.
There's a *coffin* on the second floor—for wakes!
We suck back Yeungling lager and scarf tasty pub food.

He needs a shaft of light,
something to help him through the bad moments.
I give him Epictetus.
"It is circumstances, difficulties, which show what men
are . . ."
It's not enough. Nothing is enough.

His eyes are glowing anthracite.
"I'm going to save this goddamn plant!"
"Yes, you are," I tell him.
We click glasses.

---

5   On January 22, 1959, the Knox Coal Company's River Slope coal mine
flooded. Twelve miners were drowned.

6   A nineteenth-century Irish-American secret society that resisted
exploitative conditions in the coal mines.

The Angel's Share

Early Spring, Triple Crown Bar

Sampling smoky bourbon in this 1905 Louisville bar, *VOTED TOP TEN IN AMERICA!* Catching up with an old friend; an executive, family man, and Ironman competitor. Ten thousand like him and America will recover.

Here for a conference, we talk about business, life, and the Green Bay Packers. An afternoon with him gives me books to read and ideas to reflect on for the rest of the year.

German robber barons built this hotel in the old style: Corinthian columns, frescoed ceilings, and oak paneling. Last night I strolled along Fourth Street, Frankfort Avenue, and Waterfront Park. Victorian row houses, cast-iron facades, and the shimmering Ohio River.

Our waiter, Giovanni, is a Milan boy on a co-op placement. He is learning how to run hotels. We ask him about bourbon. Giovanni sets up a line of bottles. We'll sample them one by one.

"Good bourbon is like fine wine. For each bottle, you must evaluate four things:

Candy store—*vanilla, caramel, honey, butterscotch are all common flavors;*
Fruit stand—*apple, pear, figs, dates, banana, cherry;*
Spice rack—*black pepper, tobacco leaf, nutmeg, cinnamon;*
Wood shop—*oak, cedar, pine, almond."*

As bourbon ages in oak barrels, about three percent evaporates. We call this 'The Angel's Share.' It is like, che dice, *a gift to the gods, a sacrifice we make in return for a successful harvest. You understand, no?"*

My pal tells me about his sister's baby. *"They live in Germany, tried for years to have a child, and finally succeeded. Three months old, they find a carcinoma in his brain. The doctors tell us survival rates are 'depressingly low.' Nothing to do but wait for him to die.*
"No way am I accepting that, so I get on the Net and pull in my network. Many of them are here this week. Turns out the world's best infant oncologist lives near the family. I catch him on his cell phone, we talk for two hours. That was three years ago. Today the little guy is cancer-free and doing just great. A beautiful boy. Of course, he won't remember anything."

We touch glasses. I take a sip of bourbon: *caramel, apple, black pepper, cinnamon, oak.*

The angels will have to wait.

Seelbach Hilton Hotel, Louisville

Byzantium

"WANT TO KNOW OUR CURRENT CONDITION?
WE'RE MUCKED!"

A splendid old company, founded in 1892 by a dreamer and
philanthropist who, at the end, crippled and in pain, took his
own life and left everything to the universities.
"My work is done, why wait?"
The famous logo, a yellow-red banner floating above the city,
invoked a century of vision and achievement.
Now, obsolesced by technology, desperate, in transition
the writing is on the wall: innovate or perish.

Two guys at the top
Tom, a lab rat
Bill, a steelworker's son
stanched the bleeding
long enough for another business to emerge.

They held their posts in fading light
as old structures collapsed, as health and spirit faltered.
Tom survived lung cancer and a heart attack.
He came back to work against all counsel:

"You've got to let it go, Tommy!"
Bill had seen failing steel mills
suck the lifeblood out of his family:
"I'll do my job, but I won't let it kill me!"

With earnings collapsing and Wall Street calling for blood
these guys talked Ethics
"HOLD ON HERE! WHAT'S THE RIGHT THING TO DO?"
voicing the values
of an earlier generation, an old, *OLD* school

Constantine Palaiologos,
last emperor of Byzantium,[7]

---

7   The Byzantine Empire lasted eleven centuries. Constantinople, the
Byzantine capital, fell to the Ottoman Turks on Tuesday April 2, 1453.

before the final battle, that fatal Tuesday,
asking forgiveness of his court,
"If I have ever done you wrong, forgive me."
Last sacrament, last liturgy in Santa Sophia
refusing safe passage out of his city:
instead, surging into the enemy lines, outnumbered twenty to
one.

Tom and Bill are gone now,
Battered, bruised, *unbroken.*
One is head of a small college, the other, retired to a golfing
community.
Against all odds, the company survived,
entirely changed, a new business model in place.

The yellow-red banner still floats above the city.

Kamal

He pulls up in his run-down taxi.
The front seat is littered with fast food wrappers,
the back seat with old newspapers.
Taut, thin, graying, he's thirty-eight but looks fifty.
I'm fifty. *"You look thirty-eight,"* he tells me.
He shares the cab with an Ethiopian.
"Nice guy, a very nice guy."
I notice their pictures on the dashboard,
Kamal and the Ethiopian.

He was born in Persian Kurdistan.
"Lots of hills and forest. It's cold in winter."
He looks like my Greek cousin, and might well be!
Forced to leave—*"I have political trouble . . ."*—
he's been in Canada eleven years now.
He has two diplomas and is working on a third.
He has two young kids and a young wife
who is working on a Programming degree.
Every day he drives hack for ten hours,
studies in the library for another two,
then goes home for dinner and sleep.

Kurdistan is divided among four countries.
I ask him about it.
"The Persians are not bad. The Turks are the worst."
"How do the Sunni and Shia get along?"
"We have no problems. I am not too religious."

It's a fine spring day.
I'm going in for a colonoscopy.

"It is hard driving a taxi . . ."
He tells me of encounters with drunks and other idiots.
"People are not nice here.
This woman, she is too drunk to use the banking machine.
She starts swearing at me."

I tell him of my years as a janitor.
"But you are an engineer now! I noticed your ring."
"How about driving an airport limo?"
"I don't want to be trapped. I'm not going to drive forever."

He pulls up at the hospital.
"Don't give up," I tell him.
"Never!"

Summer Regular

Sparrow Lake, North of Orillia, Ontario

Old, poor, alone
right arm hanging useless, leg in a shabby prosthesis,
mentally handicapped to top it off,
each Canada Day weekend
he takes the Greyhound
up to Blue Water Resort on Sparrow Lake.

"Good to see you again," my wife says.
"You too," he smiles.
"Didn't have a cane last year."
My kids were scared initially.
Now they're protective of him:
"Hi, Ian!"

He sits alone at dinner,
studying the birches that ring the placid lake.
He tells me about his job back in Toronto
in the government-sponsored wood shop.

"I've learned how to work the router!"

He participates in all the resort activities he can manage:
Bocce ball, horseshoes, the teddy bear workshop.

At the Friday night waterskiing show,
sky calm after heavy rain,
he takes a weathered Muskoka chair
and sits quietly in his old wool sweater
watching beautiful young bodies
soar and pirouette.

Did his mother knit that sweater for him, I wonder?
What happened to her?
He's such a valiant soul,
she must have loved him very much.

Afterwards, I watch him work his way up the hill
solo again, to the main lodge
clutching the teddy bear he's made.

An hour later, in the men's room,
I found him leaning heavily against the wall
exhausted from the effort
of just getting through the door and taking a leak.
"Can I help you?" I asked.
He shook his head.

Later he fell coming down the stairs.
We rushed to help, gathered up his cane,
the woman at the front desk holding back tears.
He brushed himself off, breathing heavily.
"I'm okay," he said.

Study Questions

1. What is a *virtue*? Draw it out.[8]

    a. Aristotle defines virtue as a *"summit between two abysses."*[9] Do you agree or disagree? Explain your answer.

2. The author suggests he'd like to help shift contemporary business discourse toward the cardinal virtues: Prudence, Temperance, Courage, and Justice.

    a. Would this be helpful? Is it realistic? Explain your answer.

3. Andre Comte-Sponville tells us that Courage is a precondition for all the other virtues. Do you agree or disagree? Explain your answer.

4. Can immoral people be courageous? Explain your answer.

    a. Under what conditions is Courage is virtue?

5. How well does your organization practice Courage? Explain your answer.

    a. What could your organization do to improve?

---

8   *The Back of the Napkin* (New York: Penguin, 2008) by Dan Roam provides insight into the power of visual thinking and tips on how to get started. Don't worry if you "can't draw." Stick figures, shapes, and arrows are fine.

9   *A Small Treatise on the Great Virtues* (New York: Henry Holt, 1996) by Andre Comte-Sponville.

II. SUNNY-SIDE UP

Tomas—"No H"

Sunny September afternoon, Chicago Botanical Garden. Our strategy session done, I stroll to the front entrance. There's my ride, an *American* taxi.

"How are *you*, SIR!" grins the cabbie, getting out to open the side door of the white SUV. "This is a very *posh* area. SERIOUS people! Deadlines, DEALS, *distractions*! I'm not like *that*. No seriousness allowed in *my* cab. I *mean* it!"

He climbs into the driver's seat and looks at me in the rear-view mirror. Nasal, somewhat whiny voice, an accent I can't place—mix of Russian, Finnish, German. Whiskers, dark glasses, and bandana—like a jovial rat.

"Don't mind at all," I reply. "Flying home to Toronto. No hurry—we don't leave for three hours."

"That's GOOD!" he exclaims. "We can take our TIME. We can *relax*."

We exchange names. His is Tomas, "no H."

"Where are you from?" I ask.

"Take a *guess*!"

I guess wrong, repeatedly.

"LITHUANIA!" he crows. "Bet you *never* heard of it!"

"Never been there," I admit. "Plenty of Baltic people in Toronto though. How long you been in Chicago?"

"*Nineteen* years. I left after the BERLIN WALL came down."

"What's Lithuania like?"

He snickers. "To tell the truth, it's *boring*. Nowadays, people want a wow! They want PARIS, ROME, LONDON! Nobody wants to say, 'Hey, I went to *VILNIUS* . . .'"

"You have a point," I laugh. "But there must be *something* in Vilnius."

"Well," he shrugs, "Vilnius has a few old BUILDINGS, a castle, and a *park*."

Mad Lithuanian, a new species for me. I don't mind playing straight man.

"Must've been tough, Tomas, growing up in a Soviet state."

"Not as *bad* as people in the West imagine," he replies. "Everybody HAD work. You had to follow some RULES. But we lived okay."

"How did you find work?"

"Well, you just *looked* in the newspaper. There were always JOBS, because they hired *three* people to do the work of one.

"So we had time to SOCIALIZE. After eight hours your work was *done*. You could go to the theater, the HOCKEY GAME, the *chess club*. It wasn't bad."

"Plenty of drinking, I imagine."

He makes a face in the rear-view mirror. "Each night they would pick up the DRUNKS. They had this truck, it was like a big black box on four wheels, and they would drive around picking up the DRUNKS. When the box was full they'd drive to the police station, strip them down, and put them in the cage. Then they'd pull out the FIRE HOSE and let them *have it*.

"INSTANT SOBRIETY!"

I laugh out loud. "Did they release the drunks after that?"

"No way!" he snorts. "THEY CHARGED THEM FOR THE WATER! The DRUNKS never had money so they had to call their WIVES. If they couldn't get money, the DRUNKS had to stay for fifteen days and do *community* service! You would see them gardening or *sweeping* the streets."

I've always found cabbies interesting. Tomas was in a class of his own.

"Were there long lineups for food?" I ask.

"We didn't suffer much in Lithuania. We always had bread. We had five or six kinds of *cheese*. Not thirty like NOWADAYS, but not bad. Who NEEDS thirty kinds of cheese? Sometimes we got oranges from *Morocco*. I think it was tougher for other SOVIET bloc countries.

"But, there was NO CRIME! Plenty of Russians are violent *gangsters*, but even they were scared of the *KGB*—the biggest MAFIA of them all!

"The SOVIETS were world *class* in only one *thing*— *surveillance* and BEATINGS! They won the *GOLD* medal in BEATINGS!"

I'm laughing so hard, I need to catch my breath. "But you had no freedom, Tomas. You couldn't start a business."

Tomas makes another face. "When the *Wall* came down, people were dancing around. FREEDOM! We have FREEDOM!"

He snickers again. "Then they realized you can't *eat* FREEDOM!"

"What's it like now?"

"Some *people*, they were smart and adapted. They are doing just GREAT. But the ones who expected the STATE to take care of them, they are having a harder time. But you know, they like to complain, even though they are much better off than they were. That's why the commies still get votes."

"How about you, Tomas, how are you doing?"

"This recession, it SUCKS, but I'm doing *okay*."

The ride is over, too quick. "You made me laugh," I tell him.

"Well, I *like* to have a GOOD time."

We settle up and shake hands, and I meander into O'Hare.

Yoopers

Improbably, this company makes money
located way up in Michigan's Upper Peninsula:
Metal fabrication, high labor content,
far from major markets and suppliers.

Norwegian, German, and French stock.
(Nick Adams[1] country—hunting, fishing, suicide . . .)

The founder is a gunslinger and gambler—an intuitive
genius.
I wouldn't want to play poker with him!
His son is a force of nature, an Olympic downhill skier and
Ironman participant. He made a big splash in investment
banking but got bored and came home. Their competitive
tension is palpable and a reason for the company's success.

I drink tonight in Falcone's Tavern,
a celebrated local joint, not unlike the Imperial Grill,
my dad's old place on Queen Street in Toronto.
Vince, the owner, lost his wife a few years back.

---

1 The protagonist of Hemingway's short stories set in the
northern woods.

"Thought I was gonna die. Then my kids put my profile on the Net . . ."
Now he's getting married again.
The food's good: hearty, unpretentious, like the people.

"YOU DO THAT FOR ME AND I'LL KISS YOUR ASS ON MAIN STREET TILL YOU BARK LIKE A FOX!"

The senior vice-president joins me at the bar.
He buffers the intense polarities of son and founder,
connects everything, makes it work:
"What do you think of Hans and Thor?" (the new hires)
I make a face. "They sound like a Norwegian comedy team!"
He laughs. *"How'd we do today?"*
"Pretty good. The team keeps getting stronger."
We plan his trip to Toronto. We'll take in a Blue Jays game, then have dinner in Greektown.
"This place is special," I tell him.

He nods. *"Yooper spirit. Not much to go around. We learn to share."*

We drink up. Vince's niece leads us to our table.
The whitefish is good tonight.

Reality & Fantasy in Old Beijing

I flew in for the weekend from Shanghai:
Cold November—off-season.
Next morning I pulled open the hotel drapes to a
sky filled with construction cranes.

The client kindly arranged a driver—Mr. Zhang
A "good old boy"—pockmarks, bad teeth, soft belly
like a Greek uncle.
He drives a tour bus in high season.

For three days he laughed, smoked, and
took swigs of high-end moonshine
I'd bought for him.

He took me to the Great Wall at Badaling.
I walked up and down the dragon's back.
Icy wind, slippery slopes,
I had to buy a winter jacket.
The only Occidental among honeymoon Chinese!

From the Great Wall, to the Forbidden City:
I walked through ornate gates of feral blue,
I wandered red-gold FANTASIES:
bronze lions and jade butterflies,

phoenix, cloud, and dragon BRIDGES,
marble white as concubine knees.
Concentric circles of desire
signed with an ancient genius.

Mr. Zhang waited for me outside, taking quiet nips
in the Mongol wind, smoking bad cigarettes.

Last night, dinner in old Beijing:
I invite Mr. Zhang and family.
We toast Greece and China
with gasp-inducing moonshine,
his wife and daughters giggling,
his son earnest in broken English.

The waitresses and kitchen staff
joke and drink with us
and take bad pictures
I still look at.

Steel Town Reborn
Pittsburgh, Pennsylvania

The sun sets on the Alleghenies.
We sit high up on Mt. Washington taking in the show.
Our client is taking us to dinner, a Steelers and Penguins fan
("We won't talk about the Pirates"), running his logistics
business well. He is eager to show off his city.

The Golden Triangle[2] is aflame, a glass and marble fantasy:
Banks, hospitals, and software houses cradled by wide rivers,
Pittsburgh panorama rivaling the Amalfi Coast.
(Who'd have thought?)

He regales us with teenage daughter stories, then talks about his town:
"When the Homestead and Thompson mills closed,
a hundred years of history ended. But we've come back."
He points out helicopters flitting past.
"Those are cancer patients, burn and trauma victims, many from out of state.

---

2   Pittsburgh's downtown, located at the confluence of the Allegheny River and the Monongahela River whose joining forms the Ohio River.

We've become a healthcare MECCA."

We drove up from the river past sagging houses, cracked alleyways, and old schoolyards. I heard ghostly children chase errant balls down hills.
I heard them sigh in the splendid churches, saw them fidget at granddad's funeral:
(ASTHMA, BLACK LUNG, MESOTHELIOMA),
the old man's twisted fingers finally still.

We looked down from time to time
on the place where satanic mills once stood
and locked-out steelworkers fought Pinkerton goons.[3]
Today, twelve silent stacks, a shopping mall, and a small museum.

Carnegie, Frick, and Magarac[4] were with us,
brooding, puzzled ghosts who didn't recognize the new Fort Pitt.[5]

---

3   In 1892, a bitter strike culminated in the Battle of Homestead, a day-long armed clash between steelworkers locked out by US Steel and Pinkerton toughs hired by the company. Eleven people died.

4   Carnegie and Frick were the nineteenth century industrial barons who founded US Steel. Joe Magarac is a legendary folk hero and a sort of patron saint of steelworkers.

5   The birthplace of Pittsburgh, built between 1759 and 1761.

Temperanza

Pescara, Abruzzi, Italy

We take the A24 east out of Rome, my wife, little boy, and I, up into the wild **Apennini,** *Italy's spine, past slate-grey peaks and ancient monasteries, down into lime-green valleys, up again toward antique hilltop towns. Past Avezzano, Pescina, Popoli, stubborn goats eyeballing us, past the exit for L'Aquila, even higher up the mountains, where a year later, earthquakes would claim a thousand lives.*

We slow down in the glorious Parco Nazionale d'Abruzzo, linger at rest stops, and breathe in the scenery. It's spring: wildflowers, a waterfall, white peaks in the distance. They say deer, bears, and even wolves are thriving. Finally, we reach Abruzzi and roll down into this Adriatic beach town, with its modern streets and buildings. (The Allies leveled it during WWII.) We drive along the central canal, make a right turn at the Adriatic, and head toward the hotel on the beach and, tomorrow, the waiting factory.

Pescara is where Italians go in summer: soft white sand, bright beach umbrellas, superb seafood. D'Annunzio was born here: poet, self-proclaimed superman, and Mussolini's forerunner. Later we'll visit the little white and mustard house where he was born.

Giancarlo is Plant Manager and our host. His rustic Renaissance face belies a gentle manner. *Multo gentile.* Like me, he has two teenage daughters. They chose not to come, I tell him. He shrugs, *"Teenagers . . ."*

We met at our strategy session in Chicago, where I introduced the cardinal virtues to a team of skeptical executives: *Prudence, Temperance, Courage, and Justice.*

"Temperanza," he told me, *"I learned this when I was seven years old. But my American colleagues, they don't understand. All they do is work."*

"I don't understand it either," I replied, resolving, again, to slow down.

First night, *Ristorante di Fabio*: dinner by the water with Giancarlo and his team, and Juergen, the Managing Director, a reflective engineer from Aachen and its splendid university. Juergen has two little boys and chats amiably with my son, Matthew.

I shoot the breeze with Franco, the Production Manager, who runs a small vineyard in his spare time. He chooses the wine, a local Trebbiano white. It's spectacular! He toasts my wife, *"Cent' anni, bella."* Mattie climbs onto his knee.

Giancarlo goes into the kitchen with Giovanni, the maître d'. They return smiling, having designed a *twelve-course* meal. Giovanni is a throat cancer survivor and sounds like Don Corleone. *"You cannot imagine what fun I had living in New York. Mulberry street, the Festival of San Gennaro—mama mia, it was fantastic!"*

Each dish is small, stylish, succulent. In between courses there is time to talk. Giancarlo jokes about my obsession with time. *"This is not so Italian, eh? When you say, 'WE START AT 8:00!', we hear, '8:00, MAYBE 9:00 . . .'"*

I laugh, but I know that tomorrow in the factory, his team will be ready. (Their morning greeting is *BUONO LAVARE!*[6])

So it goes the whole splendid evening. I look out the open window: placid sea, crescent moon, *PASSEGGIATA*[7] in full flow. Giancarlo and my wife are chatting. Franco and Juergen are laughing about something. Mattie has fallen asleep.

Back at the hotel, we realize Mattie left his shoes under the table. We call the restaurant. No problem, Giovanni will drop them off in the morning.

---

6   Work well.

7   Little evening stroll.

Hermosillo

Hermosillo, Sonora, Mexico

They work so hard in this *maquila*.[8]
They give sweet names to machines and animals:
Coqueta! Chiquita! Carmencita!
Hard done by history and the *hacienda*,[9]
they show a smiling, unsoiled face to life.

I sign in at Security and walk past saguaro cacti,
night flowers, like little pink trumpets, still open,
to the main entrance,
a cascade of ferns, fountains, and Talavera[10] tile.
High, hard desert all around:
Red sand, blue-grey mountains
all the way north to Phoenix
and west to the Pacific.

The Plant Manager learned his chops at Mazda.
Wiry, soft-spoken, reflective,

---

8   A factory that imports materials and equipment tariff-free for
assembly or manufacturing.

9   The quasi-feudal social structure of nineteenth century Mexico,
comprising a *padron* (landowner) and *peons* (laborers).

10   A fine ceramic made in and around the town of Puebla, Mexico.

he wears black cowboy boots and a straw cowboy hat with
his uniform:
cotton navy trousers and light blue denim shirt.
He's turned down big jobs in America.
"How could I leave such a plant?"
The management team mostly comes from poor families.
They're chipping away at the *hacienda.*
A fine team—worst to first in five years.
It took a while—the PADRON culture ran deep.
Hard at first to get front-line people involved.
Now I've only to suggest an idea,
a month later, they've tried it and improved it.

When Head Office announced the plant expansion
it meant security for two thousand families
and meat two or three times a week.
The stamping lines[11] burst into song,
welding robots danced to trumpets and guitars,
team leaders knocked back DON JULIO
with Presidente Fox!

Dusty roads are giving way to sidewalks,
chaparral to shopping malls.

Tomorrow it's Our Lady of Guadalupe Day.
There's a party at somebody's house.
I'm invited.

---

11 Metal-forming ("stamping") equipment.

Seattle in the Rain

I descend the Harbor Steps
and walk slippery stones in murky rain.
Pike Place Market, deserted now,
still smells of the morning's catch.

I walk past dark shops and empty bars
seeking a local joint: the Pink Door.
"Great Italian food and a jazz band!"
There's no sign—just a pink door.
An Italian diva runs the place.
Later I learn the name's a raunchy metaphor.
Wrought iron streetlights glisten-glow.
Puget Sound is a purple guitar
with glittering moonlight strings.

I come here as a *sensei.*
This company might shut its doors:
a thousand souls, caught in history's vice.
Shapers of metal for stylish machines
but China and India can do it cheaper.
If the jobs are to stay in this drizzly green oasis
the management team has to learn new metaphors:

Sensei versus Boss; *flow* versus tight control.

They're good people, they have a chance.
Maybe I can help them.
Irony—so many years I couldn't help myself!
Cut off from purpose,
I wandered foggy piers of resentment.

Ah! a pink door. I walk into an opera set:
statuary, tapestries, a hanging trapeze.
I'm told the artists perform Sundays and Mondays.

Takaoka Days

Takaoka Plant, Toyoda City, Japan

The small, immaculate taxi pulls up in front of the factory.
Our white-gloved driver, Kenji, gets out, opens the rear door, and
bows. We bow in return and pay him. No tip—he is a professional.

We check in at Security. They are expecting us.
Our hosts are small men with lined faces and dazzling
minds.
They smoke unfiltered Golden Bat cigarettes, the aroma
oddly pleasing.
They suck back single malt Scotch each night. I can't keep
up with them.
We exchange business cards. We hold theirs in two hands
and read them carefully, as we've been taught.
They are ever gracious, our senseis, no matter how thick
we are.

We begin with a brief summary of our purpose, plan, and
expected outcomes.
The factory floor is a confluence of vast rivers:
MANPOWER, MACHINERY, MATERIALS, AND METHODS.

The workers are calm, purposeful; the factory too, is
immaculate.
Beside each line: picnic tables, ping pong, shrubbery.
The Andon Board[12] above keeps score. Even a *gaijin*[13] like
me
can tell whether a production line is winning or losing.
Each minute a car leaves the factory:
beautiful, perfect, just in time.

---

12 A system used to signal quality or process problems.

13 Foreigner.

Jetlag, hangover
I can't read a word of kanji.
Karaoke again last night.
I love raw fish but am reaching my limit.
The hum of the Shinkansen[14] returning from Hiroshima.
Every scrap of land is cultivated.
In the dark forest beyond:
Demons and samurai.

After our walk-through, it's time for *hansei* — reflection.
Tea girls bring chai and strong coffee.
Our hosts light up . . .
What did we see? What does it mean?
How can we *apply* what we've learned?

This factory brought Detroit to its knees,
the unyielding focus on *what's there*
fueling the never-ending helix of improvement
as in our old aikido dojo:[15]
Lead the mind and the body will follow!
Chiba-sensei extending his arms,
leading us through core *kata*[16] over and over,
and now decades later I can do them without thinking.

---

14 Japan's so-called bullet trains.

15 Aikido is the Japanese martial art founded by Morehei Ueshiba. Dojo means "training hall."

16 Core form.

In the West, factories are said to be soulless,
yet I found poetry and paradox:
"STANDARDS FREE YOU UP!
STOP PRODUCTION—AND IT NEVER HAS TO STOP!
LEAD, AS IF YOU HAVE NO POWER!"

Afterwards, Takeda-san, the senior man,
invites me to his small house just outside Nagoya.
I bow and take off my shoes.
O-jama shimasu—sorry for disturbing.
I have brought *temiyage*,[17] sake and maple syrup.
He serves green tea.

---

17 A small gift.

Driving Into Aspen at Night

Ice sculptures like you've NEVER seen . . .
THE EIFEL TOWER! THE GREAT WALL! THE ACROPOLIS!
Mountains all around us like sleeping trolls,
double-diamond ski runs, their long white beards.
On Main Street, a subtle sucking sound:
the siphoning of tourist dollars.

I'm here on a company retreat.
They sent a car to pick me up at Denver airport
two hours and five thousand feet ago.
My driver's a skier, an odd duck.
Widower for a decade, he loses himself in day-long hikes
and extreme skiing.
In times past he might have been a mountain man.
He says he's uncomfortable with people.
What's he think of me?

Know what "cougar" means in Arapahoe?
Phantom!
The mountain tribes were laid back—not like the Apache!
To be a good racer, you gotta give yourself to the mountain.
We're at 10,000 feet. Drink lots of water!

Go easy on booze and keep aspirin handy.

I wish I had more money to tip him!

I check into the hotel.
My room is spare, plain, expensive.
There's a welcome basket on the table:
Vitamin C, aspirin, cashews.
I wash them down with wine.
I look in the bathroom mirror
turn on the TV
turn on the gas-fireplace.

WHERE ARE ALL THE CELEBRITIES?

Think

Coming home by train from New England
after several days with an illustrious company
I was struck by the simple decency
of all the people I met.
Reflective souls in doubtful times, trying to "do right."
I pushed them hard; they stayed with it,
life's foundation stones, raising sturdy children.

The Plant Manager plays blues
on a Sunburst Les Paul
and makes maple syrup.
He gives me a jar for home.

I was taught to mistrust managers.
My political science professors told me:
"FACTORIES ARE INHERENTLY FASCIST!
ALL WORK IS EXPLOITATION!"

Walking back from the vast enchanted clean rooms
I saw a portrait of the founder and his equally gifted son:
visionaries in black and white, groping toward something.
The old man sits at his desk:

Patriarch, magician, sad clown.
His credo hangs above him:

THINK!

We have done worse.

What You Do Is What You Get

Bill Hewlett and Dave Packard
flipping burgers at company barbeques
sharing their bountiful harvest.

"ENGINEERING INTERESTED US.
THE MONEY JUST CAME ALONG."

Old Tom Watson
encouraging his team to *Think*.
Young Tom betting the company
on mainframes

". . . OUT OF SHEER CUSSEDNESS!"

William Kimberly and Charles Clark:

"TREAT WORKERS AND SUPPLIERS FAIRLY.
MAKE THE BEST PRODUCT YOU CAN."

Kiichiro Toyoda and his father, Sakiichi:

"SEEK TO CREATE A HOMELIKE ATMOSPHERE.

PROVIDE CLEAN AND SAFE PRODUCTS THAT ENHANCE WELL-BEING."

George Eastman
giving his all to universities:

"MY WORK IS DONE — WHY WAIT?"

Physical

A clinic in the old neighborhood:
It's packed: Greeks, Caribbeans, East Asians.
I read the *Economist*.

"Dr. Li will see you now."
I put down the magazine
and walk past the front counter
into the examination room.

He comes in: brisk, professional
wearing a white paper mask; it's flu season:
a Chinese boy made good.

Our parents ran small businesses:
laundry, restaurant.
I like him.
He looks after my parents.

We shoot the breeze.
"Any interesting trips lately?"
I describe the Great Wall, dinner in old Beijing.
He is wide-eyed and exudes little-boy excitement.

He reviews my test results: Blood, X-ray, PSA
Then he does a physical exam
as I tell him my troubles: clients, travel, ailing parents.

He concludes his exam,
takes off the paper mask, and smiles:

"Good health! Good family! Good business!
You have some stress.
So what! No big deal!"

Study Questions

1. What is Prudence? Draw it out.[18]

2. Thomas Aquinas tells us that Prudence must govern all the other virtues. Without it, he says, we wouldn't know to what use to put Temperance, Courage, or Justice.[19] Do you agree or disagree? Explain your answer.

3. Choose a piece from this section that you find compelling.

   a. What did you like (or dislike) about the piece?

   b. Which of the virtues, cardinal or otherwise, are expressed (or violated)?

4. Draw this virtue out.

5. What *concrete* benefits does the virtue you've illustrated provide to a person or an organization?

6. Can you describe a personal or work experience which expressed (or violated) this virtue?

   a. Any reflections or learning points?

7. How well does your organization practice the virtue you've illustrated? Explain your answer.

   a. What could your organization do to improve?

---

18 *The Back of the Napkin* (New York: Penguin, 2008) by Dan Roam provides insight into the power of visual thinking and tips on how to get started.

19 *A Small Treatise on the Great Virtues* (New York: Henry Holt, 1996) by Andre Comte-Sponville.

III. THE ASS END

Heavy Industry

Union President

"Listen, kid

I got nothin' against improvement

But it's our job security you're messing with

These are our mucking jobs

We like them just the way they are

What the muck do you know about waste anyway?

I ain't scared of nothin'

They close this place, I'll be the last one that leaves

And don't give me no crap about worker involvement

You want involvement, you come talk to me

Quicker you learn that, the better off you'll be."

Production Manager

"I DON'T MIND TAKING CRAP IF I DO A BAD JOB

BUT I DON'T EVEN GET A CHANCE

I WRITE MY SCHEDULE AT 11:30 EVERY NIGHT

BY 7:00 A.M. IT'S SHOT TO HELL
AND THE SPIN CYCLE BEGINS AGAIN.

I TAKE SHIT FROM EVERYONE. I'M FLYIN' BLIND.
SPEND MOST OF MY TIME GATHERING INFO
(YESTERDAY'S MUCK-UPS: SCRAP, GRIEVANCES,
SHORT SHIPMENTS, BREAKDOWNS)
I CAN'T SLEEP, GOT A HOLE IN MY STOMACH
I COME IN SATURDAYS AND SUNDAYS
MY WIFE MIGHT LEAVE ME
MUCK IT—IT AIN'T WORTH IT
I'M GOING INTO REAL ESTATE."

Executive

"Listen, son, you're WAY OUT on a limb
I'm trying to bring you back
You don't know what you're dealing with
Improvement's all well and good
but it ain't how things go down
It ain't the way we run and that's just how it is."

Postcard from a Black Hole

My father's fallen—*hard.*
Eighty-five years old, possible broken bone, possible stroke.
We get him to EMERGENCY. They do a perfunctory exam at
Triage.
"What's the prognosis?" Nobody will say.

I can send a package around the world and track its
progress by the hour.
But nobody can tell me what's happening with my father.

We wait for an X-ray. Dad is confused, in pain.
"Can we get some painkillers?"
Nothing.
"How long is the queue? How long will we have to wait?"
Nobody will tell us.
I understand queues, the incompetence behind them.
I understand the thinking behind this place.

Everything is hidden.
Nurses chat in their pod, patients out of sight in rabbit-
warren rooms.
Invisible

My brother knows the system. "They make it hard on purpose, to discourage people from using Emergency. It's all about prevention, man. Fall into their hands, you're dead."

Hours go by. I read a magazine. My brother goes for sandwiches.

Mama is stoic; she has been through this before.

After TEN hours, Dad gets X-rayed and CAT-scanned.

The diagnosis: crushed vertebrae and a mini-stroke.

"Sorry, there are no beds."

"But where can we go?"

We scramble, find a temporary residence nearby.

They assign a social worker. She promises to make a crisis application to a nursing home the next day (and does not). With difficulty, we get phone numbers so we can follow up. (They won't give us e-mail addresses.)

I spend most of next day on the phone.

Dad's caseworker tells us she has to transfer the file—another delay.

"The residence you took him to is out of my region."

"But it's temporary, till we find a nursing home."

"Sorry, it's not my region."

What if we take him home after a few days?

"Then the file will be transferred back to me."

I hold my tongue.

The social worker calls us: *"Your dad's application is incomplete. Your doctor didn't sign in the correct place. It's illegal for me to move this application forward. Sorry . . ."*
"We put in the application six months ago. Why didn't you tell us earlier that it was incomplete?"

We're in trouble—our doctor is on vacation.
"How about the attending physician in emergency? Will he sign it?"
"He never answers his phone."
They won't give us his pager number.
There is nobody we can call, nothing we can do.
My father is in pain.

Air Jupiter

We are sitting in a long, stifling metal tube.
Flight 407 to Dallas is delayed AGAIN, same problem as last
month.
"OUR MAINTENANCE TEAM IS LOOKING INTO IT!"

It doesn't occur to anyone
there might be a *pattern* here worth investigating.

"WE THANK YOU FOR YOUR CONTINUED PATIENCE."
I didn't offer it—you *took* it.
Standard practice in this ghastly industry,
a management backwater for decades.

"WE WANT YOUR FEEDBACK!"

All right—GO MUCK YOURSELVES!

They keep us there for FORTY minutes.
The old guy in front of me has trouble breathing;
a young woman struggles with two young kids.
My temper gets the better of me.

"WHY DON'T YOU LET US OFF THIS GODDAMN PLANE?"

Finally, they relent.
We trudge back into the terminal
broken, defeated, senseless.

"THANK YOU FOR CHOOSING AIR JUPITER!"

Heavy Metal

Central Indiana

Hoosier stamping plant:
a long, grey bunker surrounded by pickup trucks.
They're losing money, the economy shifting away
from cutting metal to cutting *deals*,
from hands-on to *brains-on.*

In the shabby conference room,
the management team glares at me
arms crossed, jaws set, thick necks, big bellies
hunting jackets on hooks.
It's our first meeting—what do they think of me?
"THIS KID FLIES IN, KNOWS MUCK-ALL ABOUT OUR PLANT,
STARTS SPOUTING THIS CRAP."

In this kind of company you have to push, push, push!
till something POPS.
Sometimes you use honey, sometimes *dynamite.*

*"More people move to Indiana to study than almost anywhere.
Yet* you *act like you don't* want *to learn.*
WHAT'S YOUR PROBLEM?"

I don't mind hostility—*aimlessness* is the killer,
unexpected in the land of the Fighting Irish,
Larry Bird, and the Indy 500.

"Think the world owes you a living?
Dozens of offshore plants do what you do—cheaper and better.
Yet you sit there glaring at me *as if I'm the enemy,*
as if Brazil, China, India, Russia don't exist.
You don't like it? Too bad.
Survival is not compulsory!"

They glare some more.
Finally, we get to the end.
They gather their stuff together and walk out.
I can read their body language:
"WHO DOES THIS BASTARD THINK HE IS ANYWAY . . ."

Tomorrow, we'll tackle problems on the factory floor: machine changeover, material flow, ergonomics . . .

Unless they kill me first.

Leadership

I take the glass elevator
through purple mist and cloud
over a heartbreak panorama:
Rock, forest, El Greco sky.

Linda smiles and escorts me to the conference room.
I help myself to coffee.

Executives meander in.
"How are you? Wonderful to see you!"
Affluent men and women
in a blue and silver tower by the sea
disconnected
from emergency rooms and broken bodies,
oncology units and living ghosts,
the million lives they affect.

"Will you take us to Japan, sensei?"
The executive team likes the idea of having a sensei.
Fifteen minutes late, we finally begin.
An expensive consulting firm
has produced volumes of analysis:

Current expenditures are unsustainable!
The consulting firm's recommendation:
SLASH & BURN.

Layoffs will kill *kaizen,*[1]
work we've carefully cultivated.
Islands of excellence will drown, the best will bolt.
"I don't want to live in a box anymore!"

"This amounts to trench warfare," I begin.
"Record profits and you're laying people off . . ."

SILENCE

"You're swimming in waste. Your people are the *countermeasure.*
The past year you've seen what's possible.

"There's a moment in every person's life
and every organization's
when you have to choose between Yes and No.
This is *your* moment."

SILENCE

---

1   Japanese: to take apart and put together again; continuous incremental improvement

"YOU LACK VISION AND GUTS. YOU'RE NOT WILLING TO SUFFER."

I walk out of the conference room.
I take the elevator down,
down through purple mist and cloud
into the empty street
knowing I'll never
work with them again.

Chief Financial Officer

His face is a clenched fist. I've never met a more miserable guy. Yet my heart goes to him, a widower, raising two teenage daughters on his own.

"All expenditures are under review. I got a simple rule. If someone wants to spend money, put it on the Bill of Materials. Not just pulp, plastic, and core materials—I mean EVERYTHING, including tape and glue!

"But YOU tell me cheaper glue is messy. You say it causes quality problems and that cleanup costs exceed savings. You tell me tape cost is negligible and that we should restock based on a simple reorder trigger. You say engineers have to spend hours filling in forms for basic maintenance expenses. You tell me to go see for myself.

"WHY DO I HAVE TO GO SEE? Nobody in the factories has said anything to me. If there's a problem, how come I haven't heard? I KNOW HOW TO SAVE MONEY. I've learned NOT to trust factories, they'll bleed you dry.

"And YOU *put our cost forecasting process up on the wall and pointed out all the* WASTE—*all the unnecessary steps, double-handling, and delay.*

*"*HOW DO YOU THINK THAT MADE ME LOOK*? Our processes have worked fine for decades. We still make money, and that's all that matters!*

"Last thing: YOU *talk about* TOTAL INVOLVEMENT *and* PROBLEM-SOLVING*. What's it brought us? Show me a cost-benefit analysis.* CONTINUOUS IMPROVEMENT DOESN'T WORK IN OUR BUSINESS AND IT NEVER WILL!*"*

Sometimes things just fall apart and there's nothing you can do.

The Court of the Crimson King

Grotesques flit through the executives offices.
They scheme in shadow and draw down the company's strength.
These are the people who bring down great empires:
Rome, Byzantium, the Han Dynasty.

We puzzle them, ask odd questions:
"Who are you? What do you believe in?"
They think we're soft, and set others against us like fighting cocks.
Brutality they understand.
My colleague shows the sword—the subtlety is lost on them.

Medusa here is VP of Human Resources.
Her team is so traumatized they barely speak.
She trails venom and pop psychology. She touches younger men suggestively.
When it suits her, she plays the gender card.

Iago[2] over there, VP of Continuous Improvement,

---

2   The villain in Shakespeare's *Othello*.

Lear-jets round the continent sowing fear and discord.
This week he's with us and our Japanese sensei
who reminds me of Tohei-sensei, my long-ago aikido
teacher:
soft voice, little-boy grin, short hair immaculately combed,
tossing football players around like rag dolls.

Iago wants to get General Electric business.
We'd like to help him:
a full day with a master in their biggest factory.
Iago paces the front lobby, iPhone in his ear.
The factory management team is uncomfortable.
They don't know why we're here.
Iago hasn't bothered to share the plan.

The shop floor is chaotic:
no standards, no visual management, no flow.
Scrap and WIP[3] is everywhere. Garbage too—we pick up
what we can.
Iago is puzzled. "Don't bother. Somebody will get that."
A worker reads the paper. Another has his feet up on the
machine.
Sensei smiles, *"You have happy workers!"*
Iago sends another e-mail.

---

3   Work in process, the amount of which, in general, is inversely
proportional to a factory's capability.

On the Lear jet home, Sensei gives Iago a summary.
"Your company's activities have no meaning.
You are not ready to work with General Electric."

Iago fidgets.

"Your management team has learned to think
in a certain way over many years.
How will you change their thinking?"

Iago looks out the window.
He plays with his iPhone some more.

Later he tells us, "I don't think your *sensei* is very effective."

Delay

Blizzard:
Planes and flight crews stranded all across the continent.
I sit in Pearson Airport Terminal 1 reading Epictetus:
"UNDERSTAND WHAT YOU CONTROL—AND WHAT YOU DON'T
CONTROL . . ."

Eyes dry, neck stiff, unable to leave—or stay.
If my flight's cancelled I'll sleep in a strange hotel
and come back in the morning.
I'll somehow reschedule with the team
awaiting me in distant time zones.
Nothing to do but drink up and order another.
An Inferno[4] with no Virgil to make sense of it.
My Beatrice is far away, asleep by now, I hope.

My fellow sinners slouch on bar stools, sprawl on floors.
A diligent few have fired up their laptops.
Napoleon over there barks orders into his iPhone.

Are we just hired guns serving unseen masters?

---

4   In Dante's *Divine Comedy*, Virgil guides the narrator through the
Inferno in search of Beatrice, his beloved.

(I'm *trying* to do right. Trying to help people, save businesses and jobs.)

My cell phone starts buzzing:
a text message from number-one daughter:

Hope you got there safe. We love you, Eleanor

I love you too.

Workshop

Occasionally, you get jackasses.
They sit together, arms crossed, tight-lipped.
They know everything. They interrupt, smirking,
ready to catch the *sensei* in an error.

Commander Ozone here
tells me what's wrong with my books.
"The last line of your preface should mention the
bibliography."
"What a great idea! I'll call my publisher right away!"
High IQ, personality of a turnip, he misses the sarcasm.
He doesn't understand why everybody hates him.
Mr. Martinet over there
knows all there is to know about the subject.
"This is *way* too basic for me.
I thought this would be an *advanced* class."

His knowledge might cover the tip of a pool cue.

I remember my sensei Shin—his laughter, droll faces,
gently correcting me, accepting my ignorance,
all just part of the job.

Sorry, Shin-san.
Hope I wasn't too much of a jackass.

Industrial Fatality

He was twenty-eight
    years old
He ran the hydraulic press
        on night shift
They found him
          after break
   decapitated

The group president   got on
      the first plane to   England
I meet him at Heathrow
        We drive south on the M25
Awkwardly
    on the wrong side of the road
to visit the dead boy's parents
      It is a cloudy day
They had snow last week
         Unusual this time of year
His mother invites us
in
We sit down on
     the living room sofa

His father   sits in
                  an arm chair

She offers us   tea &   short bread
"Simon was born early on a   Thursday
He died late on a   Thursday . . ."

  There are power
        lines outside
I can hear them
              humming

His girlfriend walks   into the   living room
"He liked football.   He liked the   Premiership.[5]
Last week we   celebrated his   birthday
Now I'm   picking music for his funeral. "

The group president
                is snow
  on a windshield
              "I am so sorry . . ."
We say goodbye and
      get back into the car.
The funeral
      is tomorrow.

---

5   England's top football league.

Family Man

Heathrow airport, Terminal 3:
We board an Airbus A340.
There's a guy in front of me, shifty, cunning:
He puts two heavy bags into overhead storage bins
near the exit doors,
usurping the space of others.
Very convenient—*for him!*
but depriving two unknown people behind us
of storage space rightfully theirs.
Where will they put *their* stuff?
They'll wander these narrow aisles
jet-lagged, anxious, confused.

I catch his eye. "What do you think you're doing, pal?"

He is puzzled: *"But these people are not my family!"*

Ship of Fools

This stinking rich pharmaceutical company charges a thousand bucks a bottle for what amounts to beer. *They secured the patent a decade ago, the gift of dreamers and researchers who worked with a passion and skill the current management team could never imagine. The patent runs out in five years, after which generic manufacturers will move in and annihilate them.*

The COO is ex-Navy, but not the good kind:
Small head, long thin neck, soft, spongy torso.
He believes they have nothing to learn and that *he* is
the architect of their prosperity. *"It's all about operational excellence . . ."*

Our strategy meeting is disrupted by a power failure.
The main electrical bus has gone down—again.
They'll have to scrap the day's production—*AGAIN*.
No matter! Tomorrow is another day.

"It happens all the time," the maintenance tech told me.
"Preventive maintenance is a foreign concept here."
An auto industry veteran, scarred by plant closures,

he is their Cassandra.[6]

"How long do you think you have?" I ask the COO.

"I don't know what you mean," he responds.

---

6   In Greek mythology, Cassandra was the daughter of King Priam and Queen Hecuba. When she rejected the god Apollo, he gave her the gift of foresight but cursed her so no one would ever believe her predictions.

Bird Flying Through Snow

The road is crap.
It killed Hank Williams, Dylan Thomas, Elvis.
Will it kill an obscure consultant too?

Salt Lake City airport:
Four-day strategy session over,
I sit coughing, waiting out another delay.

It's like a hospital in here.
Fake mosaic floor, beige walls, and ceiling tiles.
The usual *services*: Brookstone, Burger King, Starbucks,
and banking machines to keep the machinery lubricated.

I eat a breakfast burrito.
The waiter is a nice kid. He recognizes me from last time.
I kill half an hour in Navajo Collectibles.
Now it's snowing. I drink chamomile tea.
I look out across the tarmac: a bird flies over the salt flats.
Everything is ugly, even the mountains in the distance,
even the bird.

An Hispanic couple sits next to me.
The guy looks uncomfortable.
The PA system is inaudible.
There is something in my eye.

Study Questions

1. Choose a piece from this section that you find compelling.

    a. What did you like (or dislike) about the piece?

    b. Which of the virtues, cardinal or otherwise, are expressed (or violated)?

2. What concrete benefits does the virtue you've illustrated provide to a person, or an organization?

3. Can you describe a personal or work experience which expressed (or violated) this virtue?

    a. Any reflections or learning points?

4. How well does your organization practice the virtue you've illustrated? Explain your answer.

    a. What could your organization do to improve?

III. THE BLUES

Gorgeous George & the Dogs of Topeka

Building a business is tough. When you start out, you take any gig you can. One of the toughest was the dog food factory in that dry county west of Topeka. On a hot, humid summer morning, we drove the rental car out of the airport, bummed out, bleary-eyed, questioning ourselves.

We were pitching to the Plant Manager, a preening bully who looked like Gorgeous George, wrestling's first cowardly villain. I'd seen George in a documentary about the sport's golden age. He wore blonde curls and a sequined robe, and strode to the ring to "Pomp and Circumstance."

George's ring valet, Jeffries, carried a silver mirror, spread rose petals at George's feet, and sprayed disinfectant round the ring before he'd enter. George wouldn't let the referee check for illegal objects until Jeffries had sprayed his hands. "Get your filthy hands off me!" he'd cry. When the match started, George cheated in every way he could.

Our George condescended to his management team and seemed annoyed by his position in life. He sniffed as we pored over his P&L,[1] looking for opportunities. We spent the rest of the day walking around the hot, sickly-sweet-

---

1 Profit and Loss statement

smelling plant, learning more about dog food than we ever cared to know.

Their number-one product was pizzle sticks—made from "100% bull penis." *A REAL MEATY SNACK!* The bull penises were braided, dried, and smoked for flavor. Everybody in the plant seemed downhearted, and I couldn't blame them.

That night we had catfish and Coca-Cola in the only restaurant in town. The waitress and fry cook were kindly people who joked and laughed in a good clean way. Life's hard, they seemed to be saying. We'll just have to do our best.

We passed a greyhound track on the way back to our motel. I wondered if the greyhounds enjoyed pizzle sticks. I knew that once their racing days were over, greyhounds had it tough too.

Gorgeous George lost to Whipper Billy Watson in March 1959 at Maple Leaf Gardens. After the match, as promised, he cut off his golden locks in front of 20,000 screaming fans and millions of television viewers. He died a few years later from complications related to prolonged alcoholism.

That night I thought about my little girls, Katie and Eleanor, asleep far to the north. I walked out past the motel parking lot, past Arby's and Taco Bell, out toward the great prairie.

The sun had set, leaving an orange, pink, and purple stain. It was still hot and humid.

I could hear the roar of the highway, and of the greyhound track.

My Grandfather Pascali

Cincinnati, Ohio

Seeking my lost granddad
I sit with Uncle John in his Cincinnati joint:
Camp Washington Chili — BEST IN AMERICA*!*

"Uncle John, what was my granddad like?"
He knows it's important.

"Your granddad was very comical.
He was always joking!"

You can't tell that from the only photo I have
and there's no description in the ship's manifest.

He arrived in America on January 10, 1921 — Ellis Island.
The job in Cleveland with cousin Eleutherios (Lefty) Zissos
didn't pan out, so he went to Cincinnati.
He worked the rail yards for fifteen years
and returned to Greece as Axis powers prepared their assault.
He died the year I was born.

All I have of you is questions.
Who were you?

What was it like living without your family
in that rooming house with all the other "bachelors"?
Saving pennies so you could buy a few acres back home,
sending money and letters with bad spelling
that the priest would read to the wife and kids by lamplight?

What did you dream about?
Did you like baseball?
What was your favorite food?
My dad didn't dance at weddings.
I wonder, did you?
Did you want to own a restaurant?
Did you shoot pool?
Were you a drinker?
If so, wine or retsina?

I walk along the Ohio river
on stones you too must have walked on.
I look up at the stars—did you?

I look up at the stars.

Blues for Bobby Fischer

BROOKLYN BRIDGE
LOOK DOWN IN SORROW
TAXIS SOUND YOUR HORNS
KING AND QUEEN REFUSE TO EAT
BOBBY FISCHER IS DEAD.

Not the vile anti-Semite
but the little kid from Brooklyn[2]
crushing his opponents
then wondering how to get home.
Not the paunchy creep in ball cap
but the stud in Armani suits
smoldering at the chessboard
like a tiger on the lawn.

Summer of '72:

---

2   Bobby Fischer, America's first chess champion, was born in Brooklyn
on March 9, 1943. His mother, "Queenie" Fischer, was a radical activist;
he never knew his father. Introduced to chess at age six, he became U.S.
champion at thirteen and a grandmaster at fifteen. Fischer took on the
Soviet chess machine and defeated Boris Spassky in the 1972 world
championship in Reykjavik.

Yorkville[3] still full of hippies and folksingers.
You kept us spellbound for July and most of August.
Chess on the front pages.
Millions buying chessboards and taking lessons.
Chess on the front pages!

I first saw you on the cover of *Life*:
languourous, elegant,
wet lips, shark-smile.

You acted crazy, made irrational demands.
"I WANT THOSE CAMERAS OUT OF HERE!"
Crazy as a fox, some said.
Spassky[4] saved you.
He defied the commissars.
"Boris Vasilievich, you must declare an ultimatum!"
"Sergey Pavlovich, I will play this match!"
His grace, a vein of silver.
Karpov[5] sadly tainted, diminished

---

3   The heart of Toronto's counterculture in the 1960s and early 1970s.

4   Spassky was world chess champion from 1969 to 1972. He saved the
1972 Reykjavik match by accommodating Fischer's eccentric behavior.
Spassky was pressured by Sergey Pavlov, head of the USSR Sports
Committee, to declare an ultimatum which would have wrecked the
match.

5   Anatoly Karpov was world champion from 1975 to 1986. He refused
to accommodate Fischer's eccentric demands and won the title by default.
Fischer withdrew from serious chess and became increasingly isolated

for not accommodating you:
"I consider the match we did not play an enormous loss."

As King, you became immobile.
You swallowed the poisoned pawns of nowhere.
You abandoned the child to anxiety's dark cavern,
the crummy cold apartment,
where he waited for Marxist Mama to come home.
"Your work is important too, Queenie!"
Madness the one opponent you could not defeat.

Gone your swirling night of bishops, rooks, and kings.
Gone your wolf lips and crazy loping stride.
GONE your unborn masterpieces.

BROOKLYN BRIDGE
LOOK DOWN IN SORROW
TAXIS SOUND YOUR HORNS
KING AND QUEEN REFUSE TO EAT
BOBBY FISCHER IS DEAD.

---

and paranoid. He died in Iceland, the scene of his greatest triumph, on
January 17, 2008.

Motor City Sadness

Detroit, Michigan

I work with the grandchildren of African-Americans who
came north
to work in this old auto plant. Old boys and girls like Greek
relatives.
Easy grins and gentle kidding:

"You got a funny walk, man.
Where do I get me a walk like that?"

"You still here, Clarence?
I thought they retired your ass!"

We work in the Assembly plant
five football fields long.
Beautiful sports cars are everywhere.
Forklift trucks whizz past.

"How we running today, Curtis?"
"We running good, my brother."

There's a cavernous mezzanine,
a graveyard of ancient robots, jigs, and dies.

They say people *live* up there.

But the plant is at risk of closing and the elders are shamed.
They can no longer provide the jobs that sustained the
community.
Kids fall into poisoned wells, vampires walk the streets.
Nature reclaims the proud boulevards. Weeds and grasses
sprout through broken sidewalks. They say deer, coyote,
and even beavers have returned.

Light Blue

The interior of this airplane
is light BLUE.
I am in business class.
My daughter's teacher is a socialist.
I must be a bastard, she says.

My socks are also light blue
and my mood.
My little boy's eyes are BROWN
and as magical
as the sun rising on Delos
on Apollo's temple there
waves lapping all around.

I am far away from him.
He weighs thirty-seven pounds
and will have his first soccer game today
while I present to another
team of executives.

A real big shot . . .

Study Questions

1. Spinoza tells us that Justice consists in the *"habitual rendering to every man his lawful due."*[6] Do you agree or disagree? Explain your answer.

2. To what degree does your organization respect and practice Justice?

    a. How might your organization improve?

3. Choose a piece from this section that you find compelling.

    a. What did you like (or dislike) about the piece?

    b. Which of the virtues, cardinal or otherwise, are expressed (or violated)?

4. Draw this virtue out.[7]

5. What concrete benefits does the virtue you've illustrated provide to a person or an organization?

6. Can you describe a personal or work experience which expressed (or violated) this virtue?

    a. Any reflections or learning points?

---

6   *A Small Treatise on the Great Virtues* (New York: Henry Holt, 1996) by Andre Comte-Sponville.

7   *The Back of the Napkin* (New York: Penguin, 2008) by Dan Roam provides insight into the power of visual thinking and tips on how to get started.

V. POSTCARDS

Scenes from the Container Industry

In and around the Middle East with Jonas, Mattias, Lena and the rest
of the management team.

1. Port Said

Korean Palace Restaurant, Port Said, Egypt

Hard to find this place. A long walk in early evening
heat. Still, Korean barbeque—who would have thought?
    Jonas, our host, orders a tray of Heineken.

"It's a simple business, really.
We move containers from point A to point B.
Sometimes we store them too, there is good money in that,
but mainly we move them.
We have 16 ship-to-shore cranes, 41 rig-to-ground cranes, and
92 rigs.
Lots of capital to get going.
We work in some pretty tough neighborhoods.
We've learned how to manage and are doing pretty well.
To get to the next level, we need to learn from guys like you.

"Thing I like about the Middle East is people take time for one
another.
Make a friend here, and they're a friend for life.

People take time for each other, not like back home.
I got sick one time, I almost died.
Everyone was away, so I called our Egyptian board member.
I barely knew him, but what else could I do?
He drove from Cairo in his own car at night.
You know that road, how dangerous it is—donkeys
everywhere.
You hit one of those, it comes through the window, and you're
finished.
Anyhow, he took me to the hospital and stayed
with me for five hours till I was out of danger.
He's a wealthy man, he didn't have to do that.
We don't take time for one another back home."

2. The Canal

Suez Canal Authority Building,[8] Port Said, Egypt

Graceful green domes, a white colonnade, built in 1869 at the inauguration. We look out onto the Canal and Port Fuad.

There's a container ship coming towards us. *Taxiarchis, Piraeus.* "It's a big one," Mattias says, "at least 5,000 TEU."[9]

---

8   The Suez Canal Authority manages the Canal on behalf of the Egyptian government. The SCA was founded in 1855 and its first president was Ferdinand de Lesseps, the French developer of the Canal.

9   Twenty-foot equivalent unit, based on the standard shipping container size.

"Ferdinand de Lesseps built the Canal," he continues. "His statue used to be on a pedestal in Port Said, but the Egyptians pulled it down. In its place they put up a memorial for the 10,000 workers who died during the Canal's construction. Can't say I blame the Egyptians. Imagine, ten years, emptying out the Sinai Desert with shovels."

"Anyhow, the British secretly bought up shares and took control of the Canal from under the noses of the French. The British kept it for eighty years and made a fortune until Nasser nationalized it in 1956. The British and French invaded, but Eisenhower yanked on their chains and they had to back off."

3. The French

George's British Pub & Seafood, Ismailia, Egypt

Old colonial streets, expansive lawns, nineteenth-century villas—not what I expected to find in the "middle of the Canal." We order fish and chips and ale.

Lena lights a Camel and tells us about the French.

"They're bastards, of course, always trying to cheat or steal.
To get paid, we have to play hardball.
One of our managers began his career with them.
At a management meeting his boss turns to him and says,
'YOU ARE AN EFFING MORON!'
The kid was shocked, but nobody else was.

This is normal practice—humiliate the juniors.
'Do you want a career in this company?' *his boss went on.*
'Then why are you paying bills on time, you effing moron?'

"They try all sorts of things.
One time, they hadn't paid us for four months.
So I held all their cargo, every last container,
till they paid with compound interest.
After that we got paid every thirty days like clockwork."

4. Cote d'Ivoire

Naguib Mahfouz Cafe, Khan-El-Khalili Market, Cairo

Egyptian coffee, cardamom; Jonas, reflective:

"Cote d'Ivoire—that's a crazy place!
They don't hate white people like they do in DRC, [10]
but every now and then, they go crazy.
Last time, about five years ago, the rebels banged on my door.
'Any white people in there?
If you're here when we come back, we'll kill you all!'

"They came back an hour later, and that's
when I knew it wasn't fun anymore.
I had to get fifty-two people out of there.
One woman hid in the trunk of her car while they trashed her
house.

---

10 Democratic Republic of the Congo.

Another guy went up on his roof.
He stayed there for two days and kept in touch by cell phone.

"The rebels, they cut off the right arms of the children
so they couldn't bear arms. Imagine that.
The French, they're bastards, but they know how to take care of
business.
They set up a line of control and told the rebels,
'IF YOU CROSS THAT LINE, WE'LL KILL YOU ALL.'
A rebel convoy did so and the French killed every last one.

"The Cote d'Ivoire Air Force had Ukrainian trainers.
They always went up with trainees.
But one day, this native pilot took off solo.
He sent a missile into a church
and killed three nurses and seven aid workers.
Within twenty-four hours the French had destroyed the entire
Cote d'Ivoire Air Force. The French got us out of there.
They're bastards, but they know what to do."

5. Salalah

Al Istanbuli Cafe, Salalah, Oman, December 2009

Oliver orders apricot-flavored tobacco. My first time
trying a shisha.[11] We had a good day at the container
terminal. It's not as hot as I expected, I tell him.

---

11 Muslim water pipe.

"It's not bad, really, except in the summer when
it's so hot my twin boys and I fry eggs on our patio stones.
Takes a while, but they fry sunny-side up.

"The Sultan is pretty good
so it's not as corrupt as other places in the Middle East.
I'm not sure democracy would work here.
Enlightened despotism isn't so bad.
The problem is the transfer of power.
What if the Sultan's son is incompetent,
or what if he has no son?

"Anyhow, Salalah's not so bad.
It really brings a family together.
Back home all we ever do is work.
Our boys are ten years old and they're learning

English, Arabic, German, and French.
Norwegian they get at home, of course.
Winter and spring are gorgeous.
There's a cool, hazy rain and everything turns green.
Just down the coast is Yemen, a real mess. al-Qaeda is active there.
We send our container ships in convoys because of pirates.
Remember that ship they took over? It was a Norwegian ship.
Our commandos went in and cleaned it up.
Nobody got hurt except the pirates."

Brazil
Sao Paolo and Guaruja

Sunday morning, 8:00 a.m. We drive a phantom-grey 4Runner out of Sao Paolo and its Italians, Portuguese, Africans, Japanese, Chinese, Greeks, and Lebanese, across the Tiete river, past the Financial district and splendid old cathedral, past Ibirapuera park and Pedro Cabral's statue, on his knees claiming the land for King Manuel, past Mad Max samba psychos sleeping amid the garbage, down the long steady slope toward Guaruja, the Pearl of the Atlantic, famous for its beaches—*Pitangueiras, Enseada, Tombo, Pernambuco,* and *Iporanga.*

It's November—spring. I am out of it. A few nights ago I was sleepless on the red-eye from Toronto. Last night it was Brazilian barbeque and a torrent of caipirinhas. I barely notice the surrounding countryside. My hosts are Portuguese-, Italian-, and Japanese-Brazilians. They're happy. Our international management conference has sold out, and the Corinthians football team won last night. I like them and their sunny, droll, haphazard culture. *"You're lucky,"* they laugh. *"There was a gang war last year. Nobody could leave the hotel!"* Four hundred people died that week, and the gangs shot down a police helicopter.

Our host and driver, Kawamura, spent three decades at Toyota Brazil, Toyota's oldest international plant. Kawamura lost his wife a few years back and now shares a beach apartment with his daughter, who is just breaking into television. I tell him he looks like Chiba-sensei, my fierce, long-ago aikido teacher.

Kawamura shrugs. *"I am an engineer and manager. I am sansei.*[12] *My grandfather left Kobe in 1908 to work the coffee plantations."*

Two months at sea, then slave wages and forced assimilation. Some of the early Japanese immigrants killed themselves: *yonige.*[13] Did Kawamura's granddad cross paths with Stavros, my maternal grandfather? Stavros worked the Sao Paolo factories for four years. He had fought in Anatolia and barely escaped the Smyrna massacre.[14] I imagine Stavros, tall, skinny, tanned, strolling this beach.

After a few hours we pull into town—condominiums rimming a crescent of white sand. We park at Kawamura's local apartment. The beaches are gorgeous, but it's still early

---

12 Third generation.

13 Japanese for "to escape at night"; a euphemism for suicide.

14 In 1922 the port of Smyrna was burnt to the ground by Kemal Ataturk's army.

and cool by their standards. *"Let's go for a beer,"* someone says.

We find a small restaurant with a good view of the water. Coconut vendors are setting up. A woman is practicing yoga. Gulls soar against a grey sky. I was hoping to see bikinis. The waiter brings beer—Antarctica *bem gelado.*[15]

My granddad never talked about Brazil. I take a sip of my beer, unable to make sense of anything.

---

15 Ice cold.

Among the Flinty Danes in Sparkling Copenhagen

Most gentle, most kind;
even their ads are self-effacing:
"ARGUABLY, THE BEST BEER IN TOWN!"

"We feel we are on the outside
vulnerable, unimportant.
Our history has been one of losses:
Norway, Iceland, Jutland.
We have learned to accommodate,
to be sensitive to Germans, English, Swedes."

But they're reportedly the happiest people on earth![16]
I like how they greet one another:
"How are you today, Anders?"
"Could be worse, Jens."

We drink Tuborg,
good beer, good company.
Our conference successful, it's time to relax.

---

16   2008 report of the Stockholm-based World Values Survey.

I look out onto Hans Christian Andersen Boulevard.
The old dreamer, cast in bronze,[17]
looks up over his left shoulder
at stardust, trolls, and fairies.
Behind him the alluring City Hall,
"modeled on Sienna's."
Later we'll walk the enchanted Tivoli Gardens
amid marching bands of children
and the tiny Prince and Princess in their golden coach.[18]

Unspoken, the threat in their midst.
But, finally, they open up.
"We are having some difficulties . . ."
Death threats, riots, embassies in flames.[19]
It's not THE LITTLE MERMAID.[20]

I take a pull on my beer. "I've heard."

"We encourage discussion, yes.
Sometimes we are slow with decisions.

---

17 The statue of H.C. Andersen in front of Copenhagen City Hall.

18 Each spring, Tivoli Gardens open to marching bands of children and an honorary little Prince and Princess.

19 In 2007 the Danish newspaper *Jyllands-Postens* published twelve editorial cartoons, most depicting the prophet Muhammad. This led to protests across the Muslim world, some of which turned violent.

20 One of Andersen's best-loved tales.

But we are a democracy.
We must stand up for what we believe in—yes?"

We raise our glasses.
I toast their kindness and decency
and ponder polarities:
Hans Christian Andersen and Muslim rioters
Globalism and medieval grievances
Hamlet and Beowulf.

Nothing is resolved
but I wouldn't bet against them.

Aachen Conference

Aachen, Germany

I walk out of the wedding cake hotel
into drizzly autumn darkness
toward the twin towers of the ancient city hall.
The old town is a medieval fairy tale:
dark streets of interlocking limestone,
sky castles in pastel dolomite,
all from the nearby Neolithic quarry.
It was Charlemagne's capital.
His tomb and golden bust adorn the cathedral,
itself splendid despite centuries of soot.
Yesterday I sat in there bathed in light.

The Seven Dwarves stagger out of a gingerbread pub.
Rapunzel blows kisses to the glistening town square.
Snow White walks by in sensible shoes.
The Dark Queen, in shiny black stilettos,
stops to light a cigarette.

I turn up my collar and reflect
on a day with German executives.
The presenters spoke in monotone:
slide after slide of PowerPoint *junk.*

Behind their Teutonic bravado,
did I detect anxiety?
Indians, Chinese, Brazilians are challenging
their carefully managed society.

"Maybe there's more to management.
Maybe we need to change."

Beautiful German technology is necessary.
But is it sufficient?
I challenged the attendees to optimize *people*.
"YOU HAVE BEEN LOOKING UP FOR DIRECTION.
YOU NEED TO START LOOKING DOWN."

Are they ready to hear it?

Rats followed the Pied Piper out of Hamelin.
Would these businesspeople heed
an obscure consultant playing a Japanese flute?

Meeting an Old Friend at the Airport

Off to Alabama to help a furniture company, I drive through the dreary Canadian tundra to Pearson Airport. I check in and get through security.

Walking past the book store I notice a new translation of Dante's *Inferno*.

What circle of hell am I in, I wonder?

I head to the bar, order red wine, and look out across the shadowy tarmac.

No cranky boatman gestures in the gloom, thank God![21]

Just Bears and Seahawks on HDTV. Settling into benign, business-traveler stupor, I recognize the Weld Shop Manager from our old Toyota plant. I motion him over for a drink.

He's on his way to Toyota Kentucky: granite face, crew cut, laser eyes that cut through steel and bullshit. I always liked him. He makes a thousand car frames a day—all perfect. Tough, fair, all a leader should be. Twelve hundred souls

---

21 In Greek mythology, the old boatman Charon ferries dead souls across the river Styx to the land of the dead.

report to him. We catch up: old pals, new model launches,
industry scuttlebutt.

I feel awkward.
He's doing what I'd have done, had I two lives:
Apprentice, *deshi*,[22] disciple of the Toyota Way.
But I'm the author-consultant,
notorious in our old plant: "the one that *got away*."

The Kentucky flight's ready for boarding.
"New plant in Mississippi," he tells me. "Watch for it."
"Say 'hi' to everyone," my parting words.
We shake hands and he heads out through porticoes of
honor.

I look out across the tarmac, and look up:
no starlight tonight.
Just Bears and Seahawks.
I order another drink.

---

22 Japanese for "student."

Mojito

March Break, 2011, Playa del Carmen, Yucatan Peninsula.

The noontime plaza's a blaze of bottle palms and bougainvillea unfurling yellow, pink, and purple blooms. Terracotta buildings cup the courtyard, none higher than four stories, per town ordinance. The sea is aquamarine, the sand white. Back home in Toronto, the days are grey, grey, grey.

The town's named for Our Lady of Mount Carmel, patron saint of Quintana Roo Province. It was originally a fishing village and last stop for Mayan pilgrims on the way to holy Cozumel, Island of the Swallows.

Yesterday my daughters and I explored the Mayan port of Tulum. We stood high up on the castle looking out over the Caribbean, walked the Temple of the Descending God, and admired the Temple of the Frescoes, the Mayan Venus adorned in still-visible blue and gold. No evidence of bloodshed. Tulum was a place of business. At Chichen Itza[23] last year, we climbed Kukulkan's great pyramid and

---

23 A spectacular Mayan city in the northern Yucatan that flourished during the late classical period. Chichen Itza's focal point is the pyramid

looked out at the surrounding jungle, imagining severed heads tumbling down the great staircase, the crowded plaza in a frenzy.

In the Mayan calendar, 2012 marks the end of B'ak'tun 13[24] and ushers in a new era. Some predict enlightenment, others the end of the world. Still others predict crop rings, alien abductions and the return of Kukulkan.

Maybe the Maple Leafs[25] will win the Stanley Cup.

I say *Hola* to Ramone and order a drink. I take a table near the fountain. My family's at the beach, our fourth year visiting this sleepy town, remote from drug wars, *sicarios*,[26] and yet more headless corpses. (Thirty-five thousand dead in the last four years.)

Three teenage boys walk past, maybe eighteen or nineteen. Tall, skinny, awkward . . .possibly as messed up as I was at their age. The lead boy wears white trunks and matching sunglasses.

---

of the sun god, Kukulkan.

24   In Mayan calendar, a B'ak'tun is a cycle comprising 5,125 years.

25   Toronto's hapless hockey team, which hasn't won the Stanley Cup since 1967.

26   Assassin.

A grackle sits on the lip of the fountain.
Blue-black, jerky bird movements, taunting yellow eyes:
"You're a jackass, you're a jackass, you're . . ."

The goof throws his beer can, which misses and splashes into the fountain. The grekel flits away, still taunting. I'm about to say something when his tall, skinny, awkward pal reaches in, pulls out the beer can, and points to the garbage receptacle.

Cozumel shimmers across the water. Mexico's drug war enters its fifth year.
Mayan gods look down on their modern incarnations. On the sea bottom, the tide stirs the remains of prehistoric creatures.
What's happening in Mexico? What's the future hold?

Ramone sets a mojito down. It's transparent, unlike everything else.

Alpha and Omega

My wife is going to the dermatologist for her annual checkup. A precaution: skin cancer runs in the family. We park in front of the clinic, walk up the stairs and into the waiting room. Not as busy as usual; hot July morning, mid-week. I check my watch: 10:25 a.m. Our appointment is at 10:30.

"Take a seat—shouldn't be too long."
I look at my wife. "Here we go."
She smiles. "Maybe they'll surprise you."
10:45, 11:00, 11:15, 11: 30 . . .
I get up, walk to the reception desk. "Our appointment was an hour ago."
"We'll call your wife in as soon as we can, sir. Please take a seat."

I sit back down, muttering. My wife shrugs, having endured many such waits with our children. But my healthcare horror stories have made her observant. She questions every procedure. "They can't manage the simplest things."

12:05—"Pamela . . ."

The dermatologist is a petite and pleasant woman. Like most specialists, she overbooks her calendar. Mustn't keep *her* waiting.

"Good you come in annually," she says, *"given your family history."*

She does a five-minute checkup: back, neck, shoulders, tops of the hands, and   ears.

"Looks good," she smiles. *"Nothing abnormal. Please ask Reception to book your next appointment. See you next year."*

The *waiting* room again. *"Please take a seat. We'll be right with you."*

"Why do we have to line up again? Why can't you book us now?"

The receptionist frowns; he is learning to be imperious. In my mind, I reach over the counter, grab him by the ear, and TWIST. But *he* didn't make the system.

Ten minutes later: *"Pamela."* We book our next appointment and get out of there.

12:35 p.m. — two hours and ten minutes.

On the way home, we pull into a quick-service restaurant. We get in the drive-through lane and order sandwiches and coffee. I grew up in a restaurant and a colleague is a QSR[27]

---

27 Quick-service restaurant.

exec. "They're pros," I tell my wife. "Visual management, standardized work, *kaizen* — they do it all."

I think of mama, dad, Uncle Louie, and all the Imperial Grill crew. Long hours, marginal wages, good food. Taking care of customers, putting us through school.

Our order is filled perfectly. We're on our way—in three minutes and twelve seconds.

Valkomen to Sweden

Arlanda Airport, Sunday, 1:00 p.m. I roll my bags toward the information desk, seeking the express train to Stockholm. Wood floors, white columns, and glass walls open to the blue November sky. Everything is clean and well-lit. There's a mural of *Mats Sundin*, former captain of the Toronto Maple Leafs. And another, of *Bjorn Borg*.

The woman at the information counter has blonde hair and speaks good English. I write her instructions down. "Jet lag," I tell her. "I understand," she smiles. I take the escalator down into the train station, buy a ticket, and sit on a pine bench shaped like a half-moon. The floor is red, the tunnel black. Here comes the train—it's yellow.

We exit the tunnel to a Nordic panorama: a forest of fir and white birch, hydro poles like Viking oars, soil and rock the glacier left behind. The train runs parallel to the highway; not much traffic today. A black-haired mom cuddles her toddler.

I think of my childhood comic book heroes: Odin, Thor, spiteful Loki. Flowing beards, horned helmets, battle clubs.

Stan Lee and Jack Kirby making magic at Marvel Comics.[28] I remember that Odin, king of the gods, decreed his son Thor must learn humility. So he placed him, without memories of godhood, into the body of a frail medical student. It always gave me hope.

Closer to Stockholm, the forest gives way to chemical and forestry company offices, IKEA outlets, municipal yards.

I get off the train at Central Station. Short walk to my hotel; it's stylish, modern, riffing on a northern lights theme. I check in, leave my bags in the room, and go exploring.

---

28 Writer-editor Stan Lee and artist Jack Kirby created Thor, Spiderman, the Fantastic Four, and other classic super-heroes at Marvel Comics in the 1960s.

(My Danish friends tell me Swedes are nasty drunks. *"They take the Malmo ferry to Copenhagen and load up their dollies with Tuborg and Carlsberg."* My Swedish friends tell me the Danes are profoundly disorganized. *"They sit around all day drinking beer."*)

I walk down Drottninggattan Avenue and cross the bridge to *Gamla Stan*, the old medieval town. All around me, seventeenth-century buildings in rainbow colors. I wander narrow lanes of interlocking stone, peek into craft stores and restaurants preparing for the dinner rush. Lonely, but there's so much to see.

3:30 p.m. The light is beginning to fade. I stumble on the Nobel Museum. Inside, I check out Alfred Nobel's bust and biography. The old boy got rich making explosives, and tried to make amends. Then I check out Churchill, Hemingway, Mandela . . .

5:00 p.m. It's dark and getting cold as I leave the museum. I slip into a souvenir shop, buy Tre Kroner T-shirts for the kids and a matching stocking cap for me. Jetlag kicking in, I get lost going back to my hotel. I end up in the Kungsgattan pedestrian shopping district, taking in store windows and Christmas lights, Swedes all around me bundled up like Canadians.

I slip into a convenience store to ask for directions. Arabic magazines and music, proprietor in white prayer cap and long-sleeved robe.

"Salaam aleichem," I offer, practicing my Port Suez Arabic. *"Min fadlek, can you help me find my hotel?"*
"Salaam aleichem," he smiles. *"You know Arabic!"* He gives me detailed directions.
"Shukran."[29]
"Mafish mushkellah."[30]

It's cold and dark outside. I pull the Tre Kroner cap down over my ears. Tomorrow, I'm meeting my Swedish colleagues in their offices in the old Stockholm Observatory. They're bright, curious, well-organized. More bureaucratic than the Danes, it's true. But then, their companies tend to be much bigger. Last year we had a traditional Swedish dinner in the rustic kitchen, then a lecture in the adjoining museum.

I find my way back to my hotel, have a seafood dinner and a nightcap at the Ice Bar across the street.

It's cold and blue in there, just like me.

---

29 Thank you.

30 No problem.

Oasis in the Sky

Fort Worth, Texas

Our first night, Lucas and I went to Billy Bob's
for ribs and Texas swing.
Tonight we sit on the second-floor patio
of this trendy Forth Worth bistro, *Reata*, which means *rope*,
the kind *vaqueros* twirled above their heads
when they came north with the herds.

We knock back margaritas, our nerves frayed.
Twelve-hour consulting days take it out of you.
There's a full Texas moon above, and all around us
Fort Worth's latest condo development, a splendid red brick
canyon.

Lucas surveys the menu.
A New Brunswick boy who once ran
North America's best metal stamping plant.
Now he's trying to teach a major new client how to do it.
Initially, consulting made him anxious.
Now he realizes there's a ton of business.
"Buffalo lasagna sounds good," he says.
"How'd we do this week?"

"We did okay," I tell him.
"Don't know how long the gig will last, though."
I'm not sure *kaizen* will take root in this company.
The topsoil is thin, dry,
like in the Hill Country southwest of here.

"I know what you mean," he replies.
We toast the Shrimper's Code:
GET IT WHILE YOU CAN — AND CAN IT WHILE YOU GET!

I joke with Bonnie, our waitress.
She is studying nursing at Texas Christian University.
She tells us about the values of the Disciples of Christ.
They sound good to me.
We order dinner and more drinks.
I sit back in my chair and take in Sundance Square:
Art Deco buildings, rooftop bars, a fine concert hall,
the regal courthouse, rose granite aglow,
the Jett Building and splendid Chisholm Trail mural.[31]

Lyndon Johnson growing up poor, greedy, haunted,
his family trapped in the harsh Hill Country:
"All my life I been running away from poverty."

---

31 A painting by Richard Haas on three sides of the Jett Building, which
portrays a cattle drive on the legendary trail that stretched from San
Antonio to Kansas.

135

I know something of his loneliness,
his anxiety and constant motion.

Lucas is a student of history,
yet we never talk about such things.
We've worked together for years.
But how well do we know one another?

Bonnie brings us two more margaritas.
Lucas and I click glasses
amid these canyons, beneath this moon
on this peculiar trail.

Study Questions

1. *"Temperance is not about enjoying less, but about enjoying better."*[32] Do you agree or disagree? Explain your answer.

2. Choose a piece from this section that you find interesting.

   a. What do you find compelling about the piece?

   b. Which of the virtues are expressed (or violated)?

   c. Can you describe a similar episode from your personal or work experience?

   d. Any reflections or learning points?

3. Describe the best place you ever worked at.

   a. Now draw it out using as few written words as possible.

4. Describe the *worst* place you ever worked at.

   a. Now draw it out.

   b. Any reflections or learning points?

5. What are the strengths and weaknesses in your current organization's culture?

6. To what extent does your organization practice the cardinal virtues? What could your organization do to improve?

---

32 *A Small Treatise on the Great Virtues* (New York: Henry Holt, 1996) by Andre Comte-Sponville.

About the Author

Pascal Dennis is a professional engineer, author, and President of Lean Pathways, an international consultancy. He developed his management skills at Toyota and has worked with leading senseis in North America and Japan. He grew up in a Greek restaurant in downtown Toronto, the Imperial Grill, which often figures in his books.

Winner of four Shingo Prizes for Excellence, Pascal is the author of *Lean Production Simplified*, *Andy & Me*, *Getting the Right Things Done*, and *The Remedy*.

Pascal studied Aikido for fifteen years and was an instructor at Toronto Aikikai. He plays guitar and piano and has been a member of several dreadful bands. He lives in Toronto with his wife, Pamela, and three children.

For more information, please visit www.leansystems.org or Pascal's page at www.amazon.com.